Animals
of Asia

Tisha Hamilton

Table of Contents

Introduction

The Gobi (GOH-bee) Desert in Asia is a harsh place. The winters are bitter cold, and the summers are scorching hot. The ground is made up mostly of small stones. The desert has mountains, streams, rivers, and forests. Early scientists didn't think that life could exist in the harsh Gobi Desert **habitat** (HA-bih-tat).

But they were wrong! In 1920, explorers found **fossils** (FAH-sulz) in the Gobi Desert. The fossils were of an early dinosaur. It was named Protoceratops (proh-toh-SAIR-uh-tops), which means "first horned face."

Now we know that more than seventy million years ago, the Gobi Desert was home to living things. Many are **extinct** (ik-STINGKT). Others live there today.

Protoceratops ▶

▲ The Gobi Desert is in Mongolia, one of the many countries that make up the **continent** (KAHN-tih-nent) of Asia.

In this book you will read about three kinds of animals that live in Asia. You will learn how each one has survived in its habitat. But each animal could become extinct. Will help for these animals come in time?

1 **SOLVE THIS**

About how many years ago was Protoceratops discovered?

Math ✓ **Point**

What information from the text do you need to solve the problem?

⭐ Ulaanbaatar

MONGOLIA

CHINA

Beijing
⭐

N
W   E
S

| 0 | | 200 Miles |
| 0 | | 300 Kilometers |

Yellow
Sea

3

Survival in the Desert

Imagine you have just landed in the Gobi Desert. You do not have Protoceratops's thick skin to protect you from the icy wind and stinging sandstorms. You do not have four wide feet to help you keep your balance on the shifting stones. You do not have large, strong teeth to chew tough trees and bushes.

Even if you did have the teeth of a dinosaur, your body probably could not stay healthy on such a diet. Unlike a dinosaur, your body has not had to **adapt** (uh-DAPT), or change, to that kind of **environment** (in-VY-run-ment).

IT'S A FACT

During the long winters, the temperature in the Gobi Desert can drop to as low as -40°F (-40°C).

4

Asia is the world's largest continent. It borders the freezing Arctic Circle as well as the tropical (TRAH-pih-kul) Indian Ocean. Both the highest and lowest places on Earth are found in Asia. It has many different habitats.

Asia

North America

▲ Gobi Desert

The Camel with Two Humps

What animals live in the Gobi Desert today? The wild Bactrian (BAK-tree-un) camel is one. And it is a good example of animal **adaptation** (a-dap-TAY-shun). Few plants grow in the Gobi Desert. There may be miles of land without any plants at all. So this two-humped plant eater makes the most of what it eats and drinks. The camel can go without food and water for several days, even while carrying loads of up to 1,000 pounds (454 kilograms).

2 SOLVE THIS

Up to how much weight can seven camels carry?

Math ✓ Point

Does your answer seem reasonable?

▲ The camel is nicknamed "the ship of the desert" because it can go so long without water.

▲ Bactrian camels

The camel's two humps are made of fat. When food can't be found, the camel's body lives off the stored fat. Then the humps begin to shrink and may even flop over. Once the camel eats, its humps plump up again.

Chomping down on a sticker bush may not sound like fun to you. But the camel's tough mouth is adapted to eating the prickly (PRIK-lee) desert plants. What if the camel gets really hungry? Then the camel might eat bones and other things, such as rope or tents.

The Bactrian camel has long thin nostrils (NAHS-trilz) that open and close. It has thick eyelashes. They help protect the camel from blowing sand. The animal's wide feet help it to stay steady on the rocky soil.

The camel sweats very little. It can change its body temperature to help save water. No other mammal can do this.

The camel has stayed alive in the desert. But it is still not safe. Humans are the camel's most dangerous enemy.

IT'S A FACT

A thirsty camel will need to drink about 30 gallons of water to fill itself up!

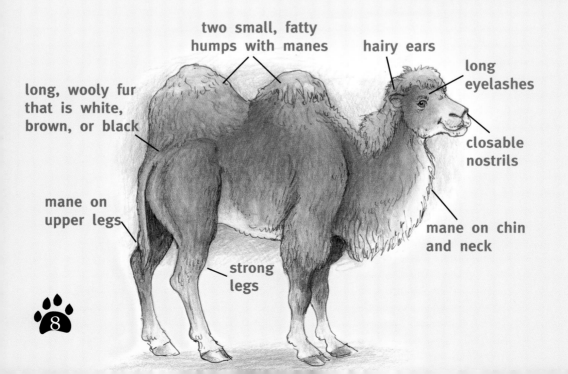

two small, fatty humps with manes

hairy ears

long eyelashes

long, wooly fur that is white, brown, or black

closable nostrils

mane on upper legs

mane on chin and neck

strong legs

The Endangered Camel

In the 1800s, hunters killed many camels. When people moved to the land, they built dams to water crops. They drilled for oil. The camels had less free land to roam and less to eat.

By 1960 the Bactrian camel had become a rare animal. In 1996 it became an **endangered species** (in-DANE-jerd SPEE-sheez). Today, the once-mighty herds that roamed throughout Asia have almost disappeared. By the year 2003, there were less than 1,000 camels left in the desert.

▲ Hunters kill camels so that these kinds of products can be made.

People are trying very hard to save the camels. Laws now make it illegal to hunt them. More land is also being set aside to keep camels protected.

Because there are so few wild camels now, there are programs to breed them. The programs may help the number of camels grow.

In July 2002, an oil company decided to reroute its pipeline. The move was done to keep the camels' habitat safe. That is a good example of how teaching people about the camel can make a difference.

People in government and business worked together. They found a way to transport, or move, oil and to help save the camels, too.

CAREERS IN SCIENCE

Zoologists (zoh-AH-luh-jists) study animals in zoos and in the wild. They also make sure that the animals get proper care so they can stay healthy. Some future zoologists work as volunteers (vah-lun-TEERZ), or helpers, at zoos while they study for a degree. They take biology (by-AH-luh-jee), zoology, and other science courses.

▼ Zoologists watch giant pandas in China.

Survival in the Bamboo Forests

Now let's go to the thick bamboo forests of China. That is where we'll find another amazing animal. It's very big, and it has fur that is black and white. Can you guess what it is?

The Bamboo Eater

If you said giant panda, you are right. Most scientists think the panda is a kind of bear. But others think the panda may not be a bear at all. They think the panda belongs in its own special group, or species, of animal. That's because there is no other kind of animal like it.

Like most bears, the panda is considered a carnivore (KAR-nih-vor), or meat eater. It will eat other animals if it can catch them. That doesn't happen often. Instead, the panda has adapted to a diet of a single plant, the bamboo. Pandas spend most of their time eating bamboo, from twelve to sixteen hours a day.

3 SOLVE THIS

How much bamboo does a zoo need in order to feed one panda for one week?

Math ✓ Point

How can you check your work?

▲ Pandas in the wild eat 25–40 pounds (11–18 kilograms) of bamboo a day. Pandas in zoos are fed about 35 pounds (16 kilograms) per day.

Strong jaws and flat ▶
back teeth help
pandas eat bamboo.

The panda has adapted in two special ways that make it a bamboo-eating machine. Its big, flat back teeth are perfect for chomping woody bamboo stalks. It also has a super-sized wrist (RIST) bone. The bone is like the bony bump on your wrist. The panda uses this bone to get a better grip on the bamboo stalk.

IT'S A FACT

Pandas do not sleep all winter. If the weather gets too cold, they simply move someplace warmer.

▲ The panda uses its "thumb" to hold onto the bamboo.

Instead of nests or dens, pandas live in a large area, or territory (TAIR-ih-tor-ee). It is about one or two square miles. The panda will probably spend its whole life in that area, roaming around, eating bamboo, and flopping down from time to time to take a nap. Except when they mate, pandas like to be alone.

4 SOLVE THIS

When pandas are born, they weigh about one-fourth of a pound. When grown, they can weigh 200 pounds or more. If a pound is 16 ounces, how many ounces does a panda baby weigh at birth?

Math ✔ Point

Is there any information you didn't need to solve the problem?

▲ This baby panda weighs 1.8 pounds (825.7 grams) and is 12 inches (30 centimeters) long.

▲ Pandas spend a lot of time alone.

Many scientists think the panda's bold coloring is an adaptation that protects it. Pandas can't see well. Their big black and white shapes make it easy for pandas to see each other. That way, they can make sure they stay away from each other!

Pandas use scent markers to communicate. They rub their scent on trees around their homes. Some scent markers mean, "Keep out! This is my home!" Some mean, "Come, say hello!"

The Endangered Panda

Long ago, the pandas' **predators** (PREH-duh-terz) were leopards (LEH-perdz) and tigers. Now their biggest predators are humans. Humans destroy their habitats in order to build. They also hunt pandas for their fur. Now the giant panda is a very endangered species.

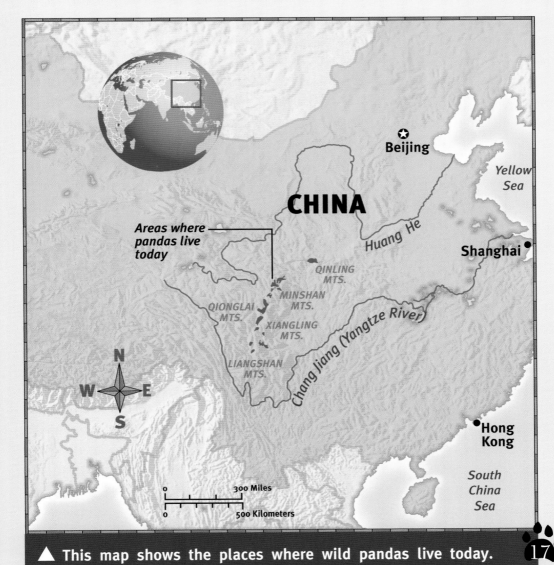

▲ This map shows the places where wild pandas live today.

Saving the Panda

Not long ago, 100 pandas starved to death when their bamboo forest died and they could not move on to a new place.

The government of China is trying to save the endangered pandas. They are growing bamboo along **corridors** (KOR-ih-derz), or pathways, that lead from one forest to another. The idea is to make it easy for pandas to move from one source of food to another. Scientists hope this will help keep the panda population growing.

▲ bamboo corridor

IT'S A FACT

There are twenty-five kinds of bamboo. Sometimes one kind dies off. Bamboo can be grown from seeds, but this takes a long time.

This giant panda ▶ lives at a panda park in Chengdu, China.

19

They Made a Difference

Zoos are also trying to save the pandas. There are about twenty pandas in different zoos around the world. The zoos take great care to **reproduce** (ree-pruh-DOOS) the panda's habitat. This helps the pandas live longer and healthier lives. It also makes it easier for scientists to study how pandas act. Then they try to find ways to help pandas in the wild.

▲ zoo habitat for pandas

▼ There are twelve bamboo **preservation** (preh-zer-VAY-shun) areas in China. These areas ensure that panda habitats are not harmed in any way.

The Good-News Panda

On August 21, 1999, a baby panda was born at the San Diego Zoo. Her name is Hua Mei (HAW MAY). She is the first panda born in a zoo to live into adulthood. In 2004, she was taken to China to live in one of the Chinese panda **preserves**. This is one way zoos can make sure pandas remain in the wild.

Survival on the Plains and in Other Forests

See if you can guess what animal this is. It's very strong. It weighs about 400 pounds (181 kilograms), but it can drag animals that weigh a ton (2,000 pounds, 907 kilograms) or more. It can leap over 30 feet (9 meters) along flat ground. It can jump 15 feet (4.5 meters) into the air! That is probably higher than the walls in your house. Can you name it now? It's the tiger.

▲ The tiger's mighty roar can be heard up to a mile and a half away. Imagine what it sounds like up close!

The tiger has what it needs to live. It has padded paws to help it to move with deadly silence. When it needs them, long sharp claws extend from the paws. Sharp teeth and strong jaws help the tiger kill with one bite. Its stripes act as **camouflage** (KA-muh-flahj). The tiger's prey can't see those stripes in the grasses.

▼ Bengal tiger ▶

The Endangered Tiger

Today there are laws against killing tigers, but they are still being hunted. Their bones are ground up to make powders and pills. Their whiskers (WIS-kerz) are used in good luck charms. Those are some reasons the tiger is endangered.

Loss of habitat is another reason the tiger is endangered. Humans clear land to grow crops. We build highways, railroads, and houses. There are fewer and fewer places for the tiger to live.

▲ Deforestation like this in Malaysia is one reason many kinds of tigers are extinct.

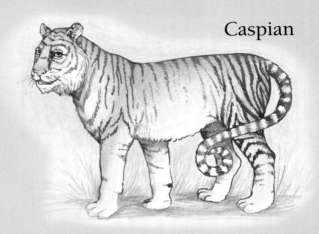

Caspian

Bali

Javan

But what happens when a large habitat is broken into smaller pieces? It separates tigers from one another. They might have to live in many different places, far away from other tigers. The smaller the population, the more likely it is to die off.

There were over 100,000 wild tigers 100 years ago. Today there are less than 7,000.

You can only see ► these kinds of tigers in pictures. They are now all extinct.

25

Saving the Tiger

People are trying to help save the world's tigers. They are trying to help governments pass strict laws against hunting. Hunters who are caught are punished.

Many groups give money to hire game wardens (WOR-denz). Game wardens watch over nature preserves and other wild areas where tigers live. Zoos also play a part in helping the tigers, just like they do for the pandas.

▲ This tiger was killed by **poachers** (POH-cherz), people who kill animals to sell their body parts.

The South China Tiger

The Chinese tiger, also named the South China tiger, is the most ancient of all tigers. All breeds of tigers started with this breed. In 1900, there were about 40,000 Chinese tigers in the wild. Now, experts believe there are less than thirty. No one has seen a wild tiger in China in more than ten years.

The Chinese people are working hard to save this beautiful animal from extinction. Zoos around China and zoologists from around the world are working to breed more tigers in captivity. The animals then can be released back into the wild. Special nature preserves in China will be the new home of the tigers. If nothing is done, the great South China tiger may disappear forever.

But there is hope. In June 2004, three South China tigers were born at the Shanghai Zoo.

27

Conclusion

It is true that humans have brought about the extinction of many species. It is also true that humans are leading the way in saving endangered animals today. Scientists are teaching us which species are in danger. By staying on top of what's going on in the animal world, we can help keep these animals safe.

✔ POINT
Talk About It
Why do you think that people are making an effort to help endangered animals? Share your thoughts with a classmate.

A Chinese researcher hugs ▶ a panda cub at the Wolong Giant Panda Bear Research Center in China.

The more people know about the dangers that animals face, the more we can work together to help save them. It is important to find new ways to let growing human populations thrive alongside wildlife.

Use the chart below to summarize some of the information you have just read. Think of other information that could be added to the chart.

Animals of Asia: Past and Present

ANIMAL	HABITAT	ADAPTATIONS	WHY EXTINCT OR ENDANGERED
Protoceratops	desert	thick skin wide feet strong teeth	maybe killed by sandslides
camel	desert	humps store fat can go without water for long period nostrils and eyelashes open and close	hunting loss of habitat
panda	bamboo forests	wrist "thumb" poor eyesight scent marking	hunting loss of habitat
tiger	plains and forests	speed power good camouflage retractable claws	hunting loss of habitat

SOLVE THIS ANSWERS

1. Page 3
Present year – 1920 = about 90 years ago
Math Checkpoint
You need the year the fossils were found: 1920.

2. Page 6
7 x 1,000 = 7,000 pounds
(7 x 454 = 3,178 kilograms)
Math Checkpoint
It is reasonable if the answer has three zeros. (For kilograms, it is reasonable if the answer is more than 2,800: 7 x 400 = 2,800.)

3. Page 13
35 x 7 = 245 pounds
(16 x 7 = 112 kilograms)
Math Checkpoint
Check your work by dividing 245 by 7 (112 by 7).

4. Page 15
16 / 4 = 4 ounces
Math Checkpoint
You don't need to know that an adult panda can weigh 200 pounds.

Glossary

adapt — (uh-DAPT) to change to fit a new living place (page 4)

adaptation — (a-dap-TAY-shun) behavior and/or body feature that helps animals or plants live in a certain place in nature (page 6)

camouflage — (KA-muh-flahj) a color, shape, or pattern that helps the wearer blend into its environment (page 23)

continent — (KAHN-tih-nent) one of the seven main land areas on Earth (page 3)

corridor — (KOR-ih-der) a long, narrow pathway that connects one place to another (page 18)

endangered — (in-DANE-jerd) in danger, especially in danger of dying off (page 9)

environment — (in-VY-run-ment) everything around a person, animal, or plant that affects its health and growth (page 4)

extinct — (ik-STINGKT) no longer living, completely died out (page 2)

fossil — (FAH-sul) part or trace of a plant or animal, preserved in stone, that lived thousands of years ago (page 2)

habitat — (HA-bih-tat) the place where a plant or animal is usually found (page 2)

poacher — (POH-cher) a person who hunts, against the law, to kill and sell animals for profit (page 26)

predator — (PREH-duh-ter) an animal that kills and eats other animals (page 17)

preservation — (preh-zer-VAY-shun) the act of keeping something unharmed, such as animals and their habitats (page 20)

preserve — (prih-ZERV) an area where animals are protected against harm (page 21)

reproduce — (ree-pruh-DOOS) to make a copy of, such as a re-creation of a special habitat (page 20)

species — (SPEE-sheez) a group of animals that are alike in certain ways (page 9)

Index